MAKING THE SKELETON DANCE

Making the Skeleton Dance

POEMS AND DIALOGUES BY
Patricia Garfinkel

To Sarah,
In appreciation for
coming to listen.
With much admiration,

Patricia Garfinkel
4/5/00

George Braziller · Publisher
NEW YORK

Refer to page 96 for a list of acknowledgments.

First published in the United States of America in 2000
by George Braziller, Inc.

For information please address the publisher:
George Braziller, Inc.
171 Madison Avenue
New York, New York 10016

Library of Congress Cataloging-in-Publication Data:
Garfinkel, Patricia.
Making the skeleton dance : poems and dialogues /
by Patricia Garfinkel.— 1st ed.
p. cm.
ISBN 0-8076-1464-5
1. Family—New York (State)—New York—Poetry.
2. Criminals—New York (State)—New York—Poetry.
3. Schultz, Dutch, 1900 or 1-1935—Poetry. I. Title.
PS3557.A7153 M3 2000
811´.54—dc21
00-020017

Printed and bound in the United States of America
FIRST EDITION

For my sons, Jef and Jon

Contents

The numbered segments are excerpts from taped conversations between the poet and her mother recorded from July 1990 through the summer of 1994.

MAKING THE SKELETON DANCE

THE BOOK OF CHILD

There are secrets that mark families, even generations.
Those who carry them live divided and troubled.
Those from whom a secret is withheld live in its shadow.

And there is passage into deeper place, to what
is hidden from oneself.

PATRICIA GARFINKEL

Making the Skeleton Dance

If you cannot get rid of the family skeleton,
you may as well make it dance.

GEORGE BERNARD SHAW

LAKE IN WINTHROP, MAINE

This lake has no name.

My parents are killing
time. They lie low,
use false names.

It is late fall, the water already
frigid, the tree limbs bare,
the shoreline crusted.
They hear footsteps.
They glimpse approaching figures.

Their shadows pace
the lake's circle.
Bury their evidence in water.

MOTHER   We went under different names. But once I made a
mistake and used our name and I thought Daddy
was going to cut my throat. He was so angry, he
wanted to kill me.

UNBORN WITNESS

Lately, my dreams are water:
I a wormlike baby,
no arms, legs, hands, ears.
But a hole somewhere cries.

I swim in the unnamed
lake in Winthrop, Maine,
snorkel for informants. My parents
wave from the far shore,
watery figures of the past
whispering in an aboriginal tongue.

Mama, you carry me here
low in your belly, late fall.
I drift in primordial soup.
My fetal skin shivers.
Secrets like ominous depth
charges ripple the placenta walls.

LULLABY

My father takes the dirty deeds,
packs off with the goods,
slips from my cross-examination.

I uncover these crimes
in fifty-year-old newspapers,
frayed film clips
of the Dutchman, Lulu,
Abbadabba, Abe the Misfit Landau,
and the Mouthpiece—
my own Uncle Dixie.

Scratching for the buried
bone, I advertise for Dixie's widow.
The ad says, "Looking for Hope Davis.
Your niece."
Too many holes bone dry.
I hire a detective.

Each time I break the silence,
uncoil some extortion deal,
unearth blood money in the closet floor,
pull a shooter and his victim
from the sack of bad dreams,
I sing Papa to sleep.

PATRICIA   Uncle Dixie knew Lucky Luciano, didn't he?

MOTHER   Oh, he knew all the gangsters—because they all wanted him to represent them. But Schultz wanted Dixie to himself. And Schultz was always against the others. Dixie knew all the Jersey guys, and the guys from Detroit in the Purple Gang, everybody, Dixie knew everybody.

PATRICIA   And so while Uncle Dixie represented Schultz, he didn't represent anyone else?

MOTHER   Not from the gangs, no.

PATRICIA   But Uncle Dixie still knew these guys?

MOTHER   Oh sure, sure, absolutely. If Daddy knew I was telling you all of this . . .

FOUND POEM:
MY MOTHER'S VOICE

What a wedding Dixie threw
for me. It was Prohibition
and the champagne flowed.
My dress was made to order,
satin and a long train.
It was such a rush, such a turmoil,
Schultz couldn't come to my wedding.

I was supposed to get gorgeous
silver and everything and I never did.
The troubles were started already
and I was promised
all kinds of things from him
and I didn't get anything.
His sister and his mother came
to the wedding, Helen and his mother,
Mrs. Flegenheimer.

I don't know why we didn't have pictures.
Daddy and I didn't even stay
for the meal. All these gangsters,
they think it's cute; we got word
they were going to kidnap Daddy.

A BEDSIDE PISTOL

You could set the air on fire
with your burnished hair,
stand tall on a bareback
circus horse trotting the ring.

Someone said the pistol
by your bed came from "Dutch,"
that you are humpbacked and white haired,
badly burned, but no details, no address.

With a photograph of glamorous pose,
raven hair, I race to catch the evidence.
You do not know I am looking.
I do not know you are hiding, only
that the trail is faint as gunsmoke.

AUNT HOPE

I grew up adoring men
at a very early age.
HOPE DAVIS

The ranch hands fought to ride with you
across New Mexico flats.
Palominos stampeded the dust
until a rancher rode his lust right up
to the stucco veranda and handed you the reins.
You were thirteen.

You lassoed diamonds
and mink coats whose ample sleeves
hung sleek and low like leather saddlebags.
One night, green-eyed and purring,
you snared my famous uncle.

Now you tell me, fifty years later,
of soothing my cries,
confessing your own fear of the dark
through my crib's wooden slats.
Like a bobcat who stalked
the old ranch, I have hunted you down
just to ask the names
of those you called the dark.

STAR SAPPHIRE

Dixie bought one big as a goiter
for his brother-in-law, my father.
Now sixty years later it is mine.

    From the gray blue luster I catch the sudden
    glint of knife in the instant between
    murderer and victim. Dixie's clients
    all carried blades—guns, too.

Dixie loved the "hot gem dealer," the gimp
with the palsied hands and confidential
news of rocks fresh from a heist,

bought them two, three at a time,
star sapphires with a high curve
like a woman's pregnant belly.

    Deep in the star's hot center, my mother
    gags on the sudden turn of events.
    Dixie, her mouthpiece brother, arrested,
    caught in a seedy apartment with a false name.

    In the stone's cloud I see
    Dixie polishing up my mother to help,
    my father pulling her into silence.

Somehow, Dixie made the switch to diamonds,
and the California coast. I was his favorite
niece, innocent of the Sapphire days.

THREE WINDOWS

1

Dutch Schultz dreams in green
bills, their silent accumulation
by shakedowns of bookies,

storekeepers, nightclub sharks.
The East River is home
to the disobedient.

His young wife tucks
two babies into suburban
sleep ten miles away.

Dutch, the daddy in their lives,
stops by sometimes with a wad
of money, sometimes with a toy,
once with a Christmas tree.

2

My uncle Dixie spins his gold
thread from threadbare shirts,
from his mother's stitches across the taffeta
and organdy of Starlight Park's rich

gentile ladies, from the broken
thread of a sister's schooling knotted
and sewn into his counsel's clothes.

He raises the Golden Rule to a new
ante while under the table gold
spills like van Gogh sunlight
to guard Dutch's crooked deals.

Dixie's gold whispers among the pillars,
flings its glittering weight against the odds.
At night he caresses its curves,
breathes heavily as he holds it near.

3

My father trades everything for blue.
The royal blue of Persian rugs
with the promise to marry Dixie's sister.

When the odds run out—Dixie handcuffed,
my mother a witness, hired guns
slithering in the grass—my father runs for cover,
a hiding place in New Jersey, a blue-collar

neighborhood to choke off his identity.
He steals into the hospital
on a starless night just to catch
a glimpse of day-old me.

MY FATHER SAID

Even the air smelled of money
on the nights of Saratoga's racing season
and everyone knew
we were Dixie's kin
there in the Piping Rock Club
riding Helen Morgan's whiskeyed voice
over the till ringing the only
song Dutch could hear.

One Sunday, in a sour
hangover, Lulu and I flew
a suitcase with the club's bank-
roll down to "the city." Out of gas,
the single engine let us down
nowhere but a farmer's empty plot,
a deadly silence
in a field with thousands of bucks.

MOTHER   Bo Weinberg was supposed to be Schultz's partner and Schultz cemented his feet in a bucket and dumped him in the East River. It made Dixie sick. Bo was the nicest, sweetest guy.

PATRICIA   But he was a gangster, Mom.

MOTHER   I don't know.

PATRICIA   He was, Mom, and so was his brother, George.

MOTHER   His mother lived in the same apartment house as Grandma, and he supported her. You'd look at him and say, what a nice guy. Always had a smile on his face.

PATRICIA   Well, Schultz didn't look like a bad guy either from his pictures.

MOTHER   Oh, he was mean, he was mean. I don't ever remember Schultz smiling. Bo used to smile. George used to smile, even that lousy Lulu used to smile. No, no, Schultz was a mean son-of-a-gun . . .

MY MOTHER CLOSED IN
WITH THE DUTCHMAN

The back bedroom a jungle,
tense, alert with animal
breath, Dutch Schultz
back and forth against small space.

He forces me
to make the phone call over
and over, dialing his rage
into no answer
imaginable to calm.

Vines hold my feet, enormous
leaves smack in the sudden wind,
a burst of obscenity and finally

the rain in torrents
until spent. The air hot but
still, he opens the door.

OBSESSED

Dutch practiced torture
like an athlete working
on his curve or crack of the bat.
Each brutality crafted to the moment,
led along a new cusp
by different sounds of fear.
Lulu and my uncle Dixie were there
the night Julie Martin got ———.
It went on for a long time,

a lot of noise about cheating,
skimming some off the top, then
Dutch stuffed his iron down
Julie's throat, the sound muffled,
blood came fast. Dutch had him
down, kicked and kicked.
The rhythm of his hard shoe breaking
Julie made Dutch light, giddy
on the precipice of new death.

There's some confusion, but
a blade, skilled and fast
as a fisherman's in Dutch's hand,
flays open the chest, carves
a heart clean from the cave.
You think it ends here,
that ecstasy is complete, but Dutch
passes around a glass of warm blood
to quench the thirst to tell.

#4

PATRICIA   Why was your telephone tapped?

MOTHER   Oh, our telephones were tapped because of
handling policy and because of Dutch Schultz.
Grandma's wire was tapped, Academy 2-1262.
Dixie's wire was tapped; and we had a special
phone in the closet that they found out about.
They were trying to get Schultz.

A PHONE IN THE CLOSET

Mama, everything collapses
to a simple question.

Was the phone
in the closet
like the top hat I wear
in the bathtub
or like a secret
Swiss bank account?

Don't tell me about the D.A.'s
tap on the other lines,
how he wired his suspicions
to search a darkness in you.

I am tapping your mind
sixty years later because
a shrill ringing persists
on the line
no one answers.

Just answer, Mama,
and let me finally
take off the top hat.

BIOGRAPHY

Biography is in the way you die.
DUTCH SCHULTZ

33 and standing at the urinal
in overcoat and gray fedora—
top of the thugs' ladder
where balance is precarious
where fast steps and quick hands
muscled him from burglar to shooter,
to Beer Baron and Numbers' Boss
to the top step:
First Enemy of the Numbered Public
where even the air is suspect,
Dutch Schultz took a .45-caliber
slug below the chest
in the Palace Chop House pissoir.

His stream stopped, the killer hands flew
to the ladder leaning backward,
cupping blood, cradling pale shocked flesh.
Whatever ladders lean against
drifted past in the last delirious rantings.
The rungs danced out of order;
a posse of cops riding slats at his back,
he grabbed for Mama over and over
to break the fall. Father McInerney
sailed in to catch this Jew on the last rung
as he murmured through 106° fever,
"Mother is the best bet
and don't let Satan draw you too fast."

PATRICIA   Where were you when Schultz was assassinated?

MOTHER   We [Daddy and I] heard it when we were in bed.
We heard that Marty Krompier was sitting in the
barber chair and he was shot but he was alive and
Schultz was shot with Abe Landau, and Lulu, and
Abbadabba. Abbadabba had a personality that
anybody could love. He had a face like the man on
the Admiration Cigar ad—a heavy, big fat face and
he was always smiling, and nobody could believe
that he was connected to the mob.

#3

MOTHER   Daddy and I were scared out of our wits. I thought
we might get killed too. I thought, God, are they
going for everybody that was connected with him.
We were scared out of our wits and we didn't dare
use our telephone because it was tapped.

MY FATHER SPEAKS
OF IMPOTENCE

The murderers come to us
in bed. Soft radio music roams
our naked bodies; my hands
roam your moist crevices
and the music stops dead
for a voice—

Dutch Schultz and three henchmen
shot in the Palace
Chop House. Marty Krompier
"sprayed" in the barber chair.

Skin tears; your skin
turns cold in my trembling.
The music again. How long
does one song last?

Forever, if the notes crack
like bullets on my back.
My body lies exposed
to the hunters who come
right to the edge
of our bed each time I feel love.

#12

PATRICIA   Between 1935 when Schultz was assassinated and
            1937 when Uncle Dixie was arrested, what did
            everybody do for those two years?

MOTHER   We had the office and we went there every day.

Stories People Tell

"Remember only this one thing," said Badger. "The stories people tell have a way of taking care of them. If stories come to you, care for them. And learn to give them away where they are needed. Sometimes a person needs a story more than food to stay alive. That is why we put these stories in each other's memory. This is how people care for themselves."

BARRY LOPEZ
Crow and Weasel

PLAYING POOL

Dixie slides the cue,
fondles its smoothness
between his fingers like flesh.

Polished balls spin
across green felt
in the low-hanging light.

Dixie, rigid as a pool cue,
plunges into moist velvet
centers of New York's sleaziest
flowers. Pool is his game,

making the balls crack
on humid night air,
racking up beads
for perfect aim, finding

the deep pocket over and over
till beads of clap
wet the sheets.

PATRICIA   When Dixie was arrested, where were you and
             Daddy then?

MOTHER   We were living in Coney Island and we heard it on
             the radio. We had a room there, just one room and
             a kitchen.

PATRICIA   You were pregnant with me.

MOTHER   Yes, and I went alone to Grandma's house when I
             heard. Daddy didn't come with me. He was afraid.
             I told Grandma and Grandpa. They lived on West
             End Avenue and it was very unpleasant.

DIXIE IN JAIL

For fifty-three years, Aunt Ev
cradled that story in the soft crook
of her memory. Ev saved her brother
Dixie's time in jail until the last,

waited for me
to grow up, to come and lift
these memories from her.

How at dawn she would leave
for the Tombs with its stench
of old urine in the corridors,
its bilious faces and raw
knuckles along the bars,

and how Dixie insisted on his delicacies.
Every day on the subway, she hauled
a shopping bag bulging
with smoked white fish and carp,
cream cheese, onion bagels, all fresh
for Dixie's breakfast.

He took the place over
like a visiting dignitary
and was a sport too. Demanded Ev buy
a dozen blankets for the other prisoners,
then sweaters, warm socks, long underwear
like drinks all around the table.

MOTHER   Dewey said to me that he got word, good word, from people that are supposed to be hired to do things, that Jimmy Hines wants Dixie to go out on bail so he can do away with him. Dewey said he would not okay the bail. And I begged Dixie not to go out. I told him, if you do, they will kill you.

PATRICIA   The Hines people would kill him?

MOTHER   They would have hired people. They knew all the Schtarkas. DON'T YOU UNDERSTAND?

PATRICIA   I'm trying to understand, Mom. Don't be mad at me.

MOTHER   Well, it's hard for me to talk about it now, very hard.

PATRICIA   It's hard for me to realize that every time I asked over the last thirty years I got no answers. So let's not argue.

MOTHER   Wait a minute. I don't know if it's important that you should know about every single detail. I really don't think so because there are a lot of things I didn't know either. So why is it so important to know every detail? At any rate, Dixie did not go out on bail.

THE MOUTHPIECE

Dixie too makes music in the underworld,
but with the quick, clear brilliance
of his mind. For the murky law of mobsters,
he fashions a tune no magistrate can resist.

Orpheus teaches Dixie to test for trust.
Turn slightly to see who follows and if
they disappear, sing, sing for your life.

Dixie's words begin to fade, the melody
confused. Orpheus dismembered,
Dixie is disbarred and his song hums
like a high-tension wire.

#28

MOTHER   We would go out at night when it was dark.

#16

MOTHER   We moved around so much it was hard to keep track
of where we were.

MY MOTHER TELLS ME
HOW IT WAS

We never lived
       We made gentile food
Anywhere more than a month
       Macaroni and cheese, white beans
Talked in whispers with the water
       And peas in cream sauce, sliced ham
Running
       Taunting ourselves with talk
All day we ate
       Of chopped chicken livers with onions
Each other's fear
       Stuffed cabbage rolls, sour pickles
In one-room flats
       We ate our own faces.

8

MOTHER   I was arrested.

PATRICIA   Where did they arrest you? Were you at Grandma's?

MOTHER   Yes.

PATRICIA   And who came for you?

MOTHER   Well, Dewey sent a woman and a man police. And they
took me down to the court, and the Judge said, "If any-
one asks you if you were ever arrested, you have a right
to say no because this is a civil arrest not a criminal
arrest. You're being held as a material witness." And
that's what happened. And from then on I had a police-
woman and a policeman with me all the time. They
used to sleep at Grandma and Grandpa's on the couch
with their clothes on. . . . They were with me for all the
time we were hiding out in the country too.

PATRICIA   Did Daddy know you were arrested? He was hiding in
New Jersey.

MOTHER   Well, the newspapers had everything, so it didn't make
any difference. He knew.

#6

MOTHER   Daddy is staying low, very low. They also wanted
Daddy to testify against Hines. Daddy used to give
Hines plenty of money—cash. Daddy did not want
to testify.

A SPINET PIANO

Papa, tell it one last time, starting
from the end. You dropped the news-
paper behind the piano, a spinet
flush against the wall. On the front
page was your photograph and a short
caption, "Wanted for questioning."

Friends hiding you took you out
visiting, using a false name
to their friends.
Earlier, you were assured no one
in that small town would know about
the trial. And you couldn't keep hiding,
going out only in darkness, only with
a hat pulled low over your eyes.

The newspapers whipped by the wind,
chase you down the last street,
you chasing your hat or the answers
shouting against the piano's raw back.

EDVARD MUNCH
PAINTS MY PARENTS

Nature is formed by one's mood.
EDVARD MUNCH

Remember Munch,
in the thick darkness
of northern winter days,
a viscount of melancholy.

He caught my parents crouched
in a crevice of their lives, knew
them, the way prisoners
know each other.

Munch holds his ears against
that shriek of blood red sunset, hears
their inner sunsets, lobs the canvas
red, orange, magenta, black
season across sinking sky.

Suffocation drops its cloak.
Breath comes anxious. Their ears dilate,
their eyes pick up high-pitched fright.
The landscape undulates, red
pushes its tense rhythm
over an unending canvas.

NAMING

Frances, do you remember
how Dutch plucked you at eighteen
from the lush speakeasy,
forced your slim, milk-white body down;
later marked your baby Anne
with Davis in the middle,
my uncle Dixie's last name?

Anne is my age,
doesn't know she got my name,
one my mother chose for me
till my father spat Davis in her face,
and I became Patricia Gail.

9

MOTHER   And of course Dewey had the top law firms in Wall Street. How many times was I taken down there to take testimony so nobody else could hear me. And these law firms that had these gorgeous staircases from the libraries to the offices.

WITNESS

In a courtroom, the witness chair is higher up,
sort of on a stage where people can see you.

MOTHER

Suddenly I can see
my mother see herself
in the mirror, the scum
in the kitchen sink. Eye surgery
has rolled back the film of years
to the prosecuting attorney who hammers
her memory for failure while a policewoman
guards my crib and detectives praise her steel
stare. I am alone with the guard in a hideout where terror
hangs like tapestries that muffle Walter Winchell, Edwin Hill
broadcast her fame till my ears are animal. Tiny fingers lock
on any blanket, hand, rattle like a life ring, Mama,
which of us is witness?

MOTHER To have people staring at me, and having the brains of the United States—Hines's people had lawyers from Washington, D.C., from all over, and everybody would hand the attorney a question to ask me. ... And I wasn't scared, but it's nerve-racking to sit with all these faces looking at you. And you know, they didn't let anybody in—when the courtroom was full, that was it. People used to come at five and six in the morning to get in the room.

APRIL 1938

I lie here barely born.
Great trees shake
their fists through the storm
around this hideout
far off in West Hampton.

Only the trees know
we are here, this frightened
fistful of witnesses
to an ordinary crime.
The scarred trunks stand
guard against the thin walls.

The policewoman has no
kind words for me.
She moves above the crib
with wooden eyes.

My grandmother strains
tea leaves from the kettle.
My parents drink tea
and listen to the rain
falling through their lives.

The uncle who got us
into this leaves his name
in the headlines.

The trees hear my cries
and bow their branches.
The tea leaves cast
their shadow of bad
news on the walls.

FOUND POEM:
MY MOTHER'S VOICE II

The police officers were telling
me how wonderful I was
on the witness stand
and that night Gabriel Heatter,
he was on every night I think,
six o'clock, one of the big stations,
he really made it
sound as if I was just the last word.

#15

MOTHER   It boggles the mind to think that people can go through so much in life and come out of it alive and sane; maybe I'm not so sane, I don't know.

THE GANGSTERS COME TO ME

As a child I thought Abbadabba
and Abracadabra were the same magic.
Fat sweetheart Abbadabba
number-crunched the ponies
to pull down ten grand a week
from tightfisted Dutch.
Handicapped those hides till
gangland scales tipped heavy
with the odds.
Blue-eyed wizard and my mother's favorite,
he was even jockeyed
onto Broadway in a Runyon play.

George, Bo Weinberg's younger brother,
and no nickname,
pulled his keeper's gun on himself.
In the smoky soup of history, he left
a hole in the evidence,
dead silence for his wife and kids.
And for me, their hand-me-down crib
where these secrets
finally burst the wooden bars.

And always the boss with a star sapphire
pinkie ring and snappy hat.
"Don't give me no Dutch or Dutchman!
To you it's Arthur, Arthur Flegenheimer,
or I'll ram my iron past

your molars, blast your throat
across the wall."
O Dutch, we all take liberties
with the dead.
But alone at night, I sense cold
metal close at hand, and clench my teeth.

MOTHER George shot himself. I'll never forget that day. God, it was awful. Grabbed the cop's revolver and killed himself because he thought he'd have to testify and he couldn't. Great big tall skinny guy, left two kids— little boy and a baby girl and a wife, for no good reason. He could have testified but he was scared. That's the way things go.

PROPHECY

"None of them will die
a natural death," said Uncle Manny;
yet not a one was stabbed or shot
or dropped into the East River
with cemented feet. All the men
in my family lived

to die of old men's ailments.
"Slick Dixie" left two sons,
William with his genius, the other
with his bent for trouble.
William hides among his books,
shades blue eyes against the past.

He strokes the cat, waits for
his brother on the lam to appear
someday on the evening news;
waits for those fugitive eyes
to lock on him like handcuffs.

FINDING MY NAME

Everybody in New York City knew
our name,
Wendroff, taught to them overnight
by news headlines, radio announcers, and
paperboys whose winter breath smoked
out cold rings of extortion, bribes
and that name.

Suddenly its simple ethnic cadence raps
on our door, slips over the window ledge,
taps our phone line, sends its irresistible
scent to those animals ready to hunt us down,
tear our flesh like Dutch who tore out
another mobster's heart while he was still alive.

One morning when I was nine my father kidnapped
our name, switched it for a safer sound.
We left the house new and clean,
with no history, with no one following.

Yesterday, I found the carcass,
the small frayed certificate. Like an animal
finding its lair, I lay down and slept there.

THE RUG

My parents bought this rug when August
was their racing season in Saratoga

    In Persia, the weaver dreamed
    blood reds, midnight blues

A rug already elegant for fifty years
in Thomas Fortune Ryan's fortune

    Bent over and over through sunrises
    of thick sweet coffee

Till the beatings of mobs-
ters threaded the loom with murder

    Fingers stiffened, cut and swollen
    from the pull of coarse thread

Julie Martin spurted blood into
Persian design on a New York hotel floor

    Cross-legged for decades in the dusty
    sun drawing the sordid dream

A mosaic of child beating
her head against unheard cries

Till the universe stops throwing
itself out and out past Persia

Like an endless spool
of violent thread

Reels in sudden reverse,
collapsing backward my time too

Light from my eyes is
sucked back by the stars.

DUTCH STEPS
FROM THE PAGE,

motions to my eyes, threatening,
reminding me of his "eye special,"
the one he played on Joe Rock,
the Bronx hood who wouldn't move
when Dutch pushed.

Dutch didn't kill him, just hung him
by the thumbs on meat hooks,
blindfolded with gauze
soaked in a brew of gonorrhea pus
and rat droppings.
Joe Rock fainted, and woke up blind.

Dutch points to my eyes, pushes me
into the foul dark that gauze makes;
in the stench of it my sight swells
open and
I can see straight down.

The Book of Child

No one ever keeps a secret so well as a child.

VICTOR HUGO

. . . or it was like a disease. One of those very complicated illnesses in which one went along for a time, unknowingly incubating whatever it was, and then, months or years later, suddenly blossomed forth with fever and chills. That early period of silent incubation was childhood. And the rest, the fever and chills, the taint of it all—that was life.

DAVID SLAVITT
Alice at 80

STRANGER

There is a stranger
in my eyes moving
across the mirror
so I cannot see
her or me but only
a twisted candle of both.

The wick has been snuffed out.
A small puddle of hardened wax
is a sign
there once was light here.

The mirror has learned
the subtle art of reflection,
a hint of the past.

CHILD

The same child turns the corner
in almost every dream without
recognition. Sometimes a frayed
hair ribbon catches the breeze.
Sometimes an organdy pinafore
slips from her shoulder.

In the farthest wrinkle
unfolding from sleep, she shrugs,
opens the palms of her small hands skyward.
Suddenly our eyes memorize each other.

PATRICIA   When did Daddy decide he was leaving us in
           California?

MOTHER   I was the last one to know. I couldn't do anything
           about it. I drove to the airport with him, and
           Grandpa sat in the back.

PATRICIA   How did he explain to me that he was going?

MOTHER   I don't know, but I said to you, Daddy is going back
           to New York because he's a lawyer and he's going to
           try to be a lawyer again and do law business. And
           you didn't like it.

PATRICIA   When Daddy decided he was leaving, then how
           did you decide I was not going to continue to live
           upstairs with you anymore? . . . How did it get
           decided that I would sleep in the bedroom with
           Grandpa?

MOTHER   I don't know. Grandma told me you were pretty
           upset. You didn't want to go to school.

GENESSEE STREET

Suddenly, the blue-tiled doorway
and Mrs. Graham our matron landlady,
whose keys unlock cellar
storage bins with black widow spiders.

The last door
is my grandparents'. They take me in.
Sarah, ferociously sewing, baking.
David, Romanian gypsy.

Sarah has the double pull-out bed
in the front room, David and I
the back bedroom. Now, the night
bedroom door blows

open a cellar suffocating
with David's breath. The only light,
draped with an old shirt.
His bed and mine, arm's distance.

My mother, alone in her flat
on the floor above us, yawns,
inspects her nail polish,
puffs the bed pillows while

hands like giant spiders
travel my skin. The arched back heaves
its shadow onto the wall.
A wet mouth on mine of stone.

PATRICIA When we came back from California and we were living in New York, I had a recurring dream. I always thought it was kind of an amusing dream because it seemed so silly. The dream was of Grandpa running in his long red underwear as if he were being chased, looking back over his shoulder, and it was near a cave or something. I remember telling people as I was growing up that I used to have this dream all the time.

THE HIDING QUILT

Someone so familiar
holds me here.

I am in a friend's, a stranger's,
not my own room.

Nausea breaks loose in my gut,
pushes up my throat.

Stain spreads the quilt's legs
and my voice is choking down recognition.

Someone rolls away
the quilt to a faraway dark

as if the bed had always been
stripped naked.

ANOTHER RECURRING DREAM

Only texture,
no figures naked or clothed,
no faint recall of urgent motion,
no sound, not even colors.

Over and over through my childhood's
unsuspecting sleep, I dreamed only
the feel of swelling, swollen,
an expanding suffocation,
going down deep into water.

Like a film blurred and gagged
from the dreamer and the dreamed,
present by its absence, riveted
by uncertainty.

This dream is blinded
by what it knows. Now, it holds me
awake, bolt upright in my bed.

PATRICIA   Didn't you ever question why I was sleeping with Grandpa?

MOTHER   It never entered my mind. I guess we thought you would feel better if there was somebody in the room.

PATRICIA   Why not Grandma? . . . Let me tell you something, Mom. My childhood is so full of holes of nonrecollection, of people not knowing what was happening to me . . .

MOTHER   What can I say to you, Darling. . . . I'm sorry.

PATRICIA   Do you understand how angry I am about my life? I hate that I am angry at you for this, Mom. Here you are at eighty-five years old, you've had a hard life. I feel terrible. I don't know where to go with my anger. I feel very guilty being angry.

MOTHER   I'm sorry. You hate me and . . .

PATRICIA   No, I don't hate you. If I did, this would be easy.

OVER AND OVER ROCKS

Tear my flimsy nightdress. How impossible
the distance to any morning
like a speck always at the horizon.

And this week, I have a fierce
groundhog burrowing right up under
my front porch, forcing himself
into the narrow space.

He is thumping, scratching to claim
his ground. I never see
him—like the mornings that hid
themselves from the endless nights.

Each window held a new
night I cannot remember.
Each day new evidence
no one wants to see. Alone

among the blind, this girl-child
hurls rocks into her heart's
tiny chambers. Her mouth
rots on the silence.

SECRETS

Each night I search
under the wing of wind
for a hidden beat, a pulse
calling out along the place
sealed from speech, numbed
against the hunger
to outgrow a mind's fortress.
The mute cry of knowing
what not to know breaks me.

The silent spirit-dances
and drumbeats of the inner
ear wait, wait.
The wind passes sharp
against my memory.

WATERCOLOR

I am giving in
to the pull of stubborn water,
to the blurred portrait that forms me.

Only my suspicions
for brushstrokes.

I cannot hold out much longer.
The lines more distinct,
the young breasts under
a plaid shirt and knitted vest.

My voice pleading, the brush
stroking me against my will.

WARNING

That deserted landscape, the man
with mean muscle and a stick.
A girl-child, long blond hair,
never turning to show her face.

The man's voice holds her to his side
like a trained animal. The rules are easy.
Just shooting practice. Nothing as violent
as bullets mind you, only rocks.

The man and the girl move past windows, each
with the face of a child, a shooting gallery
like the ones at the boardwalk in Coney Island.

This is not a game. The man forces the girl
to hurl rocks at the trapped faces. This part
has no sound, only stunned eyes, then no eyes.

Off to the side, a child's body half-buried
in leaves. The man's stick forbids
the girl to notice a small boy's
mud-caked foot still twitching.

Further on, screaming.
It is dark, others are sleeping. Someone
is hurting the girl-child every night.
Their silence is like breaking glass.

WHAT I KNOW

Notice how the children
are always small, unprotected.
And the usual, a raging man.
A frantic woman too.
The rest becomes collage.

A leather whip, thick fingers,
white knuckles, bare pink buttocks
clenched against the crack.
The chorus of scream.
A large voice spreads
the quivering thighs, paroxysms of weeping,
and the woman threatening.

The whip coils, uncoils, practices
the final picture.
The woman hears herself.
The child swallows his genitals
into darkness.

SCREAM MEMORY

The air is thick with my mother
and her mother cooking up
a remedy for my festering toe.
The circle is relentless,

driving itself
in seamless momentum.

A paste of human stool
smeared on sterile gauze
to draw the poison.
The trick of circle

is not knowing
where it begins.

I watch the toe
wound round and round
with gauze, a blur
of turning till

the street beyond
rolls distant

in the ordinary
light, while here
in the dark familiar curve,
no one enters, no one leaves.

MOTHER   And the fact that he [Grandpa] saw you, the way
           you were positioned and naked, with such a look on
           his face. It looked like happiness to me or something
           I don't know. I never saw anybody look that way—
           it was a different look.

THE BOOK OF CHILD

I rise in the cradle of my name
to clear the tight clump of redwood trees
on the California coast
a distance from girl and her secret fragments.

Dark stages an execution, a hold
on me like glittering mystery
or a dreaded ring.
Weave my moan with spider
threads. I am facedown,
whitened by deepest trees.

INCEST IN ORANGE

I am in endless
hibernation. Time
and space disappear
in the isolated dark.

I have never been
a migrant. Movement
unsettles me. I am
comfortable strumming
incest on an orange guitar.
The notes mark slow,
violent steps.

The clock ticks orange
in time with the guitar.
Its hands are bleeding.
The melody is predictably
Greek.

My stomach cartwheels
with desire.
The guitar strings tighten
around my hands like snakes.

The clock winds backward.
Its hands pass each other
in confusion. The hour
is orange. Hands reach for
each other in desperate mistake.

PATRICIA   What was I like as a child in California?

MOTHER   Well, I think you were upset because I went to work and Daddy was away. You didn't want to eat but I didn't know why.

PATRICIA   This was the time in my life when my teeth fell apart and my feet fell apart.

MOTHER   Your teeth, honey?

PATRICIA   Sure, I went to the dentist and had twenty-six huge cavities. Remember, the acid in my own saliva had destroyed the teeth. It all happened to me at the same time.

MOTHER   Oh yeah.

PATRICIA   I mean if this was not a red flag . . .

MOTHER   Absolutely, Darling, absolutely, I agree with you a hundred percent. I honestly do.

PATRICIA   Did I cry a lot?

MOTHER   No, no, you weren't the type that ever showed, no. What can I say, Darling. I'm so very sorry but I have no way of rectifying it now.

PATRICIA   I don't want you to rectify it; I want you to help me
           remember so I can piece some of this together. . . .
           I want you to tell me what I was like as a child.
           I don't have any sense of what I was like—whether
           I was a timid child, a frightened child, an angry
           child, a crying child.

MOTHER   You were a timid child, very timid and you were
           bright. . . . What can I say, Darling. I can't help you.
           You were a model child, a model child.

ESSENTIAL

Because some wounds are so unspeakable, Mother,
you speak of your father as angel.

Because you are a star witness,
you see only stars and no crimes.

Because trouble comes to you like a natural
disaster, you are not responsible.

Because your life never seems what it is,
you never need to tell.

Because I do not cry, Mother,
you say I am a model child.

WATER WEARY

In dream last night, water was
pouring across a marble slab,
no vessel to collect and hold the rush,
only a small drain, overwhelmed, choking.
Loose in the swirl, I direct
the flood. Once you have lived
in water so long your eyes shrivel.
You know the rocks by Braille.

A child again, I struggle to breathe
underwater, fill to suffocation,
forget the taste of air,
the rhythm of inhale and exhale,
the difference between land and sea.

Now I am in darkness at the bottom
of my house. Light is sucked in
by a deep red sea. I am always swimming,
I am always drowning. And the animals
are coming, furred, with gnawing teeth.
They are at my ankles, their red eyes
see in this darkness. They swim
in circles around my cries.
I go down through this life, drained
by its past, treading hard against what comes.

THE TEETH

Just the two of us now.
We wash, make coffee,
make black seams straight.
The edict to bury
within twenty-four hours
forces us along.

Just hours after,
back at the house, when my back
is turned, you grab what is left
of his mouth, the dentures,
white pegs in flesh-pink plastic,
silent in his absence,

pitch them into the garbage,
swift as a thief,
before he snaps at you
in that old game.

I watch you leave,
hear the trash chute slam,
listen for the clack of teeth,
listen for his call.

TWO FUNERALS

Some things are unexpectedly different.
The light for instance.
How its clear penetration satisfies
a search for sharpness like pinched
skin or a stubbed toe, a pain
as ballast for the heart's howl.

Only now I see the other chapel
had no windows, nor any chance
for balance with a heart hobbled,
dragging its clubfoot of unsettled lust.

Grief is the simple act of crying
when there are windows,
when they open on daylight
and a determined breeze
gathers splinters of memory.

There in the dark dream, Papa,
no song rises in my throat.
Only mirrors light the corridors
by some distant reflection, and
I become the windowless chapel.

FINDING A POSTURE

Head down like the buffalo
beating the plains,
shoulders tense against attack
from tribes and fierce lovers,
girding my dreams for avalanches.

This time in the thickened
speech of sleep, I am a car
pushing against implacable glacial ice.
Under the wheels hot with churning,
a pudding of mud, gravel,

and shreds of tinsel, still glittering,
silent in the whine of frayed rubber,
but still flashing Christmas.

HARD DIRT

Just suppose I am weary,
working to catch every drop
of water. I am guardian
of a small continent,
a slab of hard dirt
pressed in on itself,
almost impervious to water, to life.

Sisyphus nods as I haul
a wooden bucket filled with water
from a distant land. The road
is unmarked; the bucket leaks.

Just suppose this had not been true. How
would I have learned to live?

THE PAPER CARRIER'S DREAM

Dark smudges of newsprint write
a hieroglyph for my dream. Words
fall apart. Syllables break into crumbs.
The tablecloth is crawling with letters
shaken loose from the front page.
The bold headline sucks dinner into a hum
of guerrilla warfare. The Collyer brothers
are knocking at the door. One has
obituaries for eyes. The other stands
molded into multicolored comic strips.

Dream sludge rolls out on spools of morning
light. The wire-bound bundles appear
every dawn on the same street corner
like a dogged commuter waiting for the first bus.

You wonder how she will lift and carry
the heavy load. She wonders why she has
chosen the danger of darkness alone. You count
the monotonous thud of papers dropped
on doormats. She counts backward
to childhood nights of menacing shadows.
You hammer the task into each day
like an autistic child banging her head.
She whispers of doors unlocking, unknown
players bringing news of the past.

POSTMAN

The day was June, a breeze jostled
the wind chimes in a chalk clink warning,
with the postman handing over a package,
if I would just sign, a box I could not

have ordered from New York, from childhood.
The postman took my name away on the yellow
wind that lied, leaving only the ashes

of my father's life. The day stayed three
weeks in a tin box that consumed the living
room, refusing to budge. For three Junes
I held out, then took a knife to the lid.

Packaged ashes like candy in a tin,
in a plastic bag. Sweet center
of my life in loose shale, gray shards

rub and shift in my whispering hands,
your heart's faint screech in my fingers,
wind chimes, wind chimes on the doorbell's ring,
the postman rubbing our names against each other.

SCATTERING
MY FATHER'S ASHES

Mute as justice at a lynching,
on the courthouse grounds
we shuffle our feet against
a stone sky.

Only after our hands scoop
into the gray mound of shale
can we defy the delicacy of "ashes,"
spit out "bones,"
from our heart's marrow.

Afterward, my sons and I, tried
by bone dust, not knowing how
to wipe our hands
and suddenly his words,
"Let's have a drink."

The way a judge slams
his gavel, I bang
the empty death-tin on the polished bar,
order two beers and a double scotch.

The business of bones
takes bravado. Jef shakes the last
shards on the flagpole base. We leave
his canister on the bar's dark wood.

Names and Identities

MY MOTHER
Rose Wendroff, changed to Rose Walker.

MY FATHER
Hyman Wendroff, changed to Wynn Walker, attorney, handled the cash and assignments in Dixie's law firm.

DIXIE DAVIS
My mother's brother, born Julius Richard Davis, Uncle Dixie, attorney for mobster Dutch Schultz.

HOPE DAVIS
Dixie Davis's wife, Ziegfeld Follies girl, Broadway showgirl, Aunt Hope.

EVELYN ZUPNIK
Born Evelyn Davis, my mother's younger sister, Aunt Ev.

SARAH DAVIS
My maternal grandmother.

DAVID DAVIS
My maternal grandfather.

DUTCH SCHULTZ
Born Arthur Flegenheimer, 1930s mobster in New York City, Bronx Beer Baron during Prohibition.

THOMAS DEWEY
New York City district attorney, Republican presidential candidate in 1948 running against Harry Truman.

JIMMY HINES
The most powerful of the Democratic district leaders in New York City, head of New York's Tammany Hall.

FRANCES FLEGENHEIMER
Dutch Schultz's young wife.

ANNE DAVIS FLEGENHEIMER
Dutch Schultz's baby daughter.

BO WEINBERG
Born Abe Weinberg, 1930s mobster, Dutch Schultz's partner, killed by Schultz.

GEORGE WEINBERG
1930s mobster, brother of Bo Weinberg, Dixie Davis's best friend, committed suicide.

LULU ROSENKRANTZ
Born Bernard Rosenkrantz, 1930s mobster, Dutch Schultz bodyguard.

ABBADABBA BERMAN
Born Otto Biederman, 1930s mobster, manipulated the racetrack betting odds for Schultz.

Grateful acknowledgment is made to the following publications where some of the poems included in this collection first appeared:

California Quarterly—"Watercolor"

Devil Blossoms—"Obsessed"

From the Red Eye of Jupiter (Washington, D.C.: Washington Writers' Publishing House, 1990)—"Paper Carrier's Dream" and "Incest in Orange"

George Washington Review—"April 1938"

Hungry as We Are: An Anthology of Washington Area Poets, ed. Ann Darr (Washington, D.C.: Washington Writers' Publishing House, 1995)— "Genessee Street" and "Hard Dirt"

Lip Service—"Three Windows," "Dixie in Jail," and "The Teeth"

Negative Capability—"Warning"

Orphic Lute—"Recurring Dream"

Pittsburgh Quarterly—"Postman," also appeared in *Women and Death: 108 American Poets,* ed. Jesse of the Genesee and Dorian Arana (Ann Arbor, Mich.: Ground Torpedo Press, 1994)

Poetry Bone—"Finding My Name," also appeared in *Winners: A Retrospective of the Washington Prize,* ed. Karren Alenier, Hilary Tham, and Miles David Moore (Washington, D.C.: The Word Works Press, 1999)

Shades of Gray—"Child"

Visions International—"Biography"

WordWrights—"Book of Child," "The Rug," and "Unborn Witness"

WPFW 89.3 FM Poetry Anthology, ed. Grace Cavalieri (Washington, D.C.: The Bunny and the Crocodile Press, 1992)—"A Spinet Piano"